Writing Naked

Writing Naked

Poems

Coleen Marks

Copyright © 2019 by Coleen Marks

All rights reserved. No part of this book may be reproduced, stored, or transmitted in any form or by any means—mechanical, electronic, recording, photocopy, or other means—without the written permission of the author.

Publisher: PrintPOD Publishing
Hillsborough, New Jersey

Editor: Jacqueline Flamm
Production Coordinator: Michael Aslett
Production Editor: Kymberly Rosenthal

Contact: printpodpub@gmail.com
Phone: 908-917-3400

Printed in the United States of America

First Edition 2019

ISBN: 978-0-578-47604-9

For Marvin
whose constant love
and encouragement endures

*Remembering yourself in the past
is how you know who you are today.*

Patricia Bauer

*It is never too late
to be who you might have been.*

George Eliot

Contents

It's Time	10
Flow	11
Let's Be Blunt About This	12
My Father's Gift	13
And This is Ben's Eldest	14
The Black Sheep	16
The Bucket and the Dipper	17
The Classroom Drill	18
That First Proposition	19
Hard Ball	20
The Walk Home	21
Sgt. Gomez	23
Mister Hoostie	24
Writing Naked	25
Art Show	26
That pile on the museum floor	27
Today is Bloom's Day	28
On the Fourth Floor	29
The Boy Sat on My Lap	30
Rubbish	31
Debris – NY Port Authority	32
Iceland	33
Oh, Brave New World	34
I Will Arise and Go Now	35
My Grandfather	36
Come Say Goodbye	37
Civilities	38
Enough	39
Hard to Believe	40
Wild Woman	41
Traveling the Midwest	42
Exit Interview	43

A Shift	46
The Lesson	47
Note to Grandson	48
Revisiting Frost	49
How Do You Think of It?	50
Crossing Paths 1975	52
At Ninety-One	53
Frail	54
Don't Ask Me to Remember	55
Acknowledgments	57

It's Time
    for Grandma Moses

You, the ultimate late bloomer
have inspired me to believe that I always
have time to join the conversation,
send my work out to see the world.

Hey, I'm only seventy-five.
Yet, there is twilight in the atmosphere
and for me, it is such truth
I always do better with deadlines.

Flow

We sink into deep silence.
Stories come that
tell us who we are.

They sit on the see-saw
between too simple
too complex.

Ideas swing into the
hide and seek of words
as we try to find their place.

Time slips away.

Let's Be Blunt About This

> *Poetry is a bird, prose is a potato*
> *Billy Collins* – On Craft

No strangers are
interested in your story.
Only those in your workshop
who know you.
You can't just open a vein
and bleed all over the page.

Poetry is crafty.
A prose avoidance system
that gives the reader
no excuse to stop.

Not a line can snooze.
Each awake and making
tidy pirouettes, rhythms
more real than words.
Never equal to the task.

My Father's Gift

It was arbitrary as a gust of wind.
He would pause in our daily struggles
and look around like an owl
pull us children into the moment
of the things in that room
or out across a rolling fresh mown lawn
or while slicing into that first
ripe tomato from the garden,
and ask, *I wonder what
the poor people are doing?*

And This is Ben's Eldest
for Benjamin Franklin Marks

Waiting outside the change house to carry your lunch pail home
I remember all those miners' black faces pouring out of the lift.
Your tales of childhood in the hardscrabble sharecropping South.
First and always a carpenter, how you taught me the many
different kinds of wood as we rubbed the beauty in.
But most of all your humor right to the end,
when you tell my sister, *Don't buy the shovel yet!*

The silence came so quickly, for one just sixty-six.
Cancer on Valentine's Day, gone by Memorial Day.
This dying a most singular thing, and one
more day too much when the pain comes.
Knowing the crop was lost, you said it was enough
and went down under that rich dark soil
you were always looking for, leaving behind
just the usual things: jackets on hooks, shoes in a closet,
pocket knife, photographs in a wallet, seven children
and your smile on my face.

And I finally visit your stories here in this
Tennessee River valley, where time and dust
float slowly in the southern heat.
Our family gathers bringing dishes they are known by.
And cousins say, *You're OK for a Yankee 'cause you're kin.*
They all hear slower than I speak, so I repeat myself
to these familiar unknown faces.

Next day, Uncle Doug's Chevy pick-up
carries us down into narrow dirt roads as he
explains how he got the *calling*
to preach at revivals and I smile
my Northeastern smile.

We pull up to the beginning a tin-roofed
sharecropper's shack leaning like age
near Bluewater Creek and Uncle Doug says,
Over yonder there's Brown Wilson's fields
where your daddy worked his last crop
before going North, and I feel
that rich dark soil of dreams
that lowdown cool of creeks.

The Black Sheep

And now, how is it you have come
so far from your clan?

Maybe it was because you had left
the cult of the Virgin
to undress for paintings,
the breath of hot kisses
in the bruised smell of mint.
Married a Jew.

Or, being the oldest gave you
a distance, put you in charge,
your Father's right hand.
Plus, you had always hated their gossip,
made a pact with Peter Pan,
your face buried in books.

Or, found you could never really network
with those who bought the ladder,
kept their lives in résumés,
could not see past the bottom line,
believed that bank books
were the true measure of worth.

Or, because you became Joe Friday,
trying to sort out Rashomon,
searching for words with answers
somewhere out on the edge.

The Bucket and the Dipper

My father was a font
of old Southern sayings,
wry comments on behavior,
He must have hid behind the door
when they were handing out brains.

I found these helped me glide above
taking too many things to heart.
As Daddy always said,
Someone whose bucket is empty
has to get their dipper in yours.

So, the snarky insult,
the pointed knife of put-down,
the grimace sent to sabotage my smile,
become an image of the other,
empty bucket, dipper in hand.

The Classroom Drill

It is a spring morning
when it goes off,
that stuck siren sound.
Missiles would be coming,
they said.

It is a world when
Atomic is a brand name
and Ground Zero is explained
in Life magazine with
radiation bands in bright
rainbow circles around NY.
We would have twenty minutes,
they said.

So, we sixth graders
are rushed into the hall
a line of silly geese
to crouch down tight against
those boring green tile walls.
Told to grip our hands
behind small heads,
like prisoners of war.
To protect us from flying glass,
they said.

The signal comes, all clear
this is a test, this is only a test,
they said.

That First Proposition

It was years ago   yesterday
just as I told it to his next-door neighbors
after I escaped   ran to their house that night.

That, hours ago, I had tucked
two little girls safe in bed.
That, they came home drunk
from a day at the ballgame
far away where the Bronx was.
She, stumbling like a stricken doe,
he, helping her to the sofa, where
she went dead to the world.

Knowing he still had to drive me home,
my mind backed out, got things ready.
When his eyes got large and looked
straight through me. He said he
wanted to check on the children
then called for me to come upstairs,
grabbed me in the dark hallway
squeezed me to him tight like a snake,
his drunken breath hissing in my ear,
You want to don't you.

Nun-sheltered   under fourteen,
all the things they never tell you
still hidden in their dark corners
yet I knew   I didn't want to.

Hard Ball

There was not much for children
to do in a mining camp.
But below the grid of thirty or so
twin company houses
they had built a real ball field.

Always a pick-up game
using the spectrum of ages/sexes
who showed up that day
so one needed to be careful
choosing up sides.

We climbed our hands up the bat
to see who could pick first
for we all knew who was best.

The Walk Home

Mornings always ran late.
The walk home after school
was another matter in this
rural company town
of miner's children,
everyone called the Camp.

Our veneer of socialization
not yet thickened
strong animal instincts
could smell the mouse and knew
the dog you had better let lie.
As the day's pent-up storms
would thunder off the bus
a lesson in aggression
could be had at any time.

Mostly the killing tongue
deflected with those pat retorts
sticks & stones or *every knock a boost.*
However, being a real smart ass
could get your teeth handed to you
and I always had a way with words.
So, when nasty Kenny picked on my sister
he dealt with the eldest of our Irish clan.

When we got home
my Mother was beside herself,
*I expected to get a call about
one of my sons beating up someone,
not my daughter.*
But then – she was an adult,
had forgotten about how
the fate of the world
depended upon your standing up!

Sgt. Gomez

We all called him *Spanky*
for he was short like his father
lost forever down a mineshaft
when he was just a twig
that grew a little wild,
and his single mother thought the Army
just the thing for pruning.

He left when only seventeen
whip smart and muscular,
I was fourteen, with girlhood wafting
on a flirting breeze.
And the Army proved just the thing
for it became his father
gave him brothers   and a war.

His breeze blew briefly by again.
Now I was seventeen
of more shapely interest
to a seasoned ranger
on assignment to West Point.
Teaching fresh lieutenants
how to wage a jungle war.

Too soon he followed duty back
was lost on some
nameless numbered hill
they had taken once before.

Today a breeze is blowing down
this long black granite wall.
I find I never knew
your first name was *Gelacio*.

Mister Hoostie

He was from the camp,
its streets of matching
Company houses laid out
in a neat grid below the mine
he'd spent his life in.

Alone now, way past working
and *given to the drink*
our parents said.
Mostly sad and quiet
to my memory.

In the hills beyond the Camp
our farmhouses had outbuildings
for storage and the like.
He took to staying
in one of my aunt's next door.

And we gave him food,
warm winter clothes,
took him to the places
you must go, and then
he left, our parents said.

This is rural life,
cities far more complicated.

Writing Naked
> *for Adolf Konrad*

An artist who could truly capture clouds.
Those large romantic white ones
with all their shadowed roundness
floating weather-less against
a Canaletto blue, forever.

He even created a painting full
of clouds on a Magritte high ceiling
holding an elaborate chandelier
in one of those strange
Victorian homes he was known for.
Each front lawn a ghostly garage sale
of period furniture and family photographs
staring out at you

And on those days when things look up
because I see that sky, recall
the beginning, his encouragement
that pastel of a warm afternoon
me posed, writing on his last rose
of summer blanket, hiding nothing.

Art Show

That first coffee was warming hands
on a Labor Day, Saturday morning.
Artwork crowded the sidewalks
all around Washington Square.
Up ahead the slow clot of judges
came toward us down the
artery of shapes and colors.
When it all stopped as if
a director had yelled – cut!
People parted like the waters
as a loud singing rounded the corner
confidently striding in the body
of a tall black man, and we
all froze like rabbits to watch.

This New York moment
adorned in a harlequin of rags
was full out singing with
a gap-toothed grin that
struck me so comically I laughed.
He stopped abruptly
approached my low lawn chair
bowed gracefully, gently
took my hand and kissed it,
then spun around and went on
singing down the sidewalk.

That pile on the museum floor

is the latest work and assaults us
with the romantic tendencies
of a dehumanized yet elevated merchandise
pulled down from the attic
brought in from the street.

It is art as a Duchampian commodity
of self-consciousness
full of post-modern literary suggestions
steeped in traces of empathy
transfigured from the existential quotidian
of our techno-mechanical lives.

This ennobled work is so
garbled in Magrittean mystery
we need the writing on the wall
to interpret its higher more chaotic
post-Dada comments that rest
upon the geometric shadow
of Divine Intention.

An exhibit meant to jolt us past
the direct impress of life and send us
beyond the vulgar tasteless limits
of our exploding media culture hype;
then exit, through the gift shop.

Today is Bloom's Day
for Evelyn

The sun is rising on our street
of postwar ranch houses
young City marrieds first purchased
with a VA mortgage and two dollars down.
My time for a wandering walk.
When I see her Barbie painted face
sitting on the neighbor's lawn
reading his newspaper.

In her driveway, next to mine
sits a VW bus the Collyer brothers
could have left there
and her scrawny cat sits posed
in an Egyptian prayer for food.
She approaches wearing
an unknown Picasso
wrapping her heart of gold.
This morning she recites Tennyson,

Break, break, break
On thy cold grey stones, O Sea!
And would that my soul could utter
The thoughts that arise in me

Then speaks to me with eyes
that peer from a Gypsy's glass
I'm nervous, she says, *today is Bloom's Day*
and I'm to read from Ulysses at the college.
I say, *Yes, again yes, I understand – yes.*

On the Fourth Floor

A girl is crouched
snail curled into a chair
fisted fingers tight against her teeth.
They watch her   in shifts.

A John Doe brought in from the night
his whole life a bad fall
can remember no place   no name.
His comic   *Say what's*   make us laugh.

A trembling gray twig of a man
inches down the desk to beg
the price of some cigarettes.
They tell him   *Call your family   a friend.*

An un-homeless woman sits watching
across the long table at lunch.
Staring from her vacant rooms she asks,
You gonna eat all that food?   We share.

Out of habit   the white uniforms
all shout at us slowly.
Then push the button
to let us out the door.

The Boy Sat on My Lap
after Gwendolyn Brooks

We caring points of light
took our Dick & Jane to troubled Trenton
every Wednesday afternoon to help
Saint Alma with her *Project Lift.*

Downstairs, my dear friend Dr. Weinstein,
counseled streetwise single moms
on how to cope with being dealt a lousy hand
and for the first time, learn what nurturing
was supposed to be, could do.

Upstairs, we cared for their turbulent tornados
fresh from the sugar rush of danger
just walking home from school.
I could see Tyree, only seven,
had a special cloud of need upon his face.
I sat him on my lap and listened
to how he had seen his teenage Uncle
shot dead in front of him the day before.

I hugged and rocked a childhood
already elsewhere.

Rubbish

In this late afternoon light
full of slanted shadows I see
you, tucked asleep, curled
up on a rolling rubbish bin.
Your small legs dangling down
like blue-jean vines
against its earthy orange.

How does it come to this?

Did your decisions slip
the net of home,
tough-loved out of reach?

Or, have you escaped a house
so strewn with abuse and neglect
your tears finally left for the street?

Cradled on this garbage
do you sleep peacefully
away from the dilemmas
of a pocket-change life?

Dream of a love that
cannot bear your absence?

Or, are you listening to our footsteps
as we pass by and leave you
on the great bottom of this city?

Debris – NY Port Authority

Did you see it on the six o'clock news?

They had shown the troubled homeless man
curled on the floor in his last crawl.

Well I was there
on my way to work.
I saw him grab the gun
from the cop's holster.
It jerked and jumped in the air
as I dove behind a news-stand
through all the screams and bullets.

Flat on the floor staring
at coffee spills, newspapers,
discarded cigarettes
and all I could think of,
all I could think of was
my God, my face is on
this filthy floor.

Iceland

The people here are pure back to 640 AD
along with meticulous medical histories
a giant Petri dish of un-noisy DNA that might
help us discover, then cure, all our ills.

The experiment began around 1996
now half of their three hundred thousand souls
have had their human genome mapped
as we seek to crack the code for our kind.

DNA can also tell if you like crossword puzzles,
have an artistic mind, as well as
your risk for breast cancer, Alzheimer's.

And as sequencing keeps scaling up to cheaper
will they find those among us
as different as we are from the apes,
predict the tinker, tailor, beggar man, thief?

We now slide down this slope into debate,
must face the question, how will we handle it
when we really know who we are?

Oh, Brave New World

We are in the wild west of media riding out of the cloud.
The Information Highway carrying us through
cunning curves into echo chambers constructed to maximize
our buying pleasure with *you might also like*
stalking our digital footprint, creating algorithmic bubbles
holding narrow views never challenged.

Today, the chalk talk of teachers is boring
next to the clickbait, the pop-ups of the funhouse
in our children's hands. Yet, just type in any question
and all the volumes of mahogany Britannica,
every word in unabridged Merriam-Webster
flies off the shelf to scroll upon your screen.

Yet *Alt-Right* trolls are posting how
nobody understands that brown shirkers
are getting all their tax dollars when it's
their white lives that aren't working out.
And who knew that faceless sock-puppets
would astro-turf fake news espouse
old racial epithets as still the truth
pronounce *Jews will not replace us.*

So, I am trying hard to keep my ideals and like Anne Frank say,
In spite of everything I still believe that people are really good at heart.
But Facebook   Twitter   YouTube   Instagram
give voice to all these empty barrels so loud, crass
and undeniably stupid that our better angels need
to get out there, raise their voices and begin to sing.

I Will Arise and Go Now

I fly in through the veils of morning
to search for Innisfree.
A long ravine runs down
the generations I carry back
to these green hills and streams
and I think of my never-met
great-grandmother seen only sepia-toned
resting her hand on my
mother's childhood.

And, Erin-Go-Bragh is forever
for the landscape seems
rural as when she left.
The rock-strewn bogs, the lakes,
the forty shades of blue-green seas.
I see the soft pale faces, with shining rust hair
play harps and fiddles, pipes and drums
still sing the songs of rebellion
and dance her reels and jigs.

In Dublin's fair city I squeeze
into a bee-loud bus next to a character
right out of, *The Quiet Man*.
And he says, *Ah, you're here from America,*
and I share from my deep heart's core
that I am the first to return, and he says,
in his soft lilting brogue,
Ah, you've come home now!

My Grandfather
for Jack Mullen

His life mostly at sea, on battleships
shooting through two world wars.
I was the first Grandchild.
And he taught me to name
every part of his model sailing sloop
before I started school.
High on his shoulders I watched
it tack and catch the wind
on Prospect Park Lake.

Many times, I heard how his birth records
were lost in the San Francisco earthquake.
How he could always lie about his age.
Would join the Navy at only sixteen
sail off to see the world.
Yet he stopped watching baseball
when Jackie Robinson began to play.
Love and praise mix with haunting missteps,
prepare me for a complicated world.

Come Say Goodbye

They called my brother and the word went out,
Your mother does not have much time.
We, her seven different stories, gathered together,
waited for the last breath of an everyday life,
not long enough, and well we knew, with its regrets.

Now comes the dreaded whispering wake
(I did not vote for, nor will ever have)
and I must bring along my four-year-old grandson,
who would always go with me, bring his toys,
and play with his great-grandmother
at the nursing home.

We join the line weaving up to the open casket.
I kneel and say a Hail Mary (out of habit),
so wish her in Heaven, yet doubt there is one.
Then, my grandson steps up onto the riser,
reaches in and gently pats her folded hands,
says loudly, *You sleep now, Grandma.*

Civilities
for Mistie

First, do no harm.

I am without incantations
for your terminal disarray.
Time, quiet as a wristwatch
is suddenly Big Ben
in this now short story,
the one where you die.

And how do you speak to
the end of a story?
Conversation is a sea,
you must keep moving, stay afloat
but our words grow heavy
sink into silences.

Today, with no forward,
I reach back into the corners
of our music, our poetry
as the day becomes a split screen
of grief and work and I demand
some gesture from the sky,
some gray, some rain.

Enough

>*for Philip Levine who knew,*
>*"What Work Is"*

I was fresh out of High School.
It was just a summer job   still
I only lasted a week.

Working on that line of machines
the feeding in   the getting out
the red-hot wires burning grids
into black foam speaker fronts.

With all the standing   bending   fumes
I decided their minimum wage wasn't enough
to keep me at *this kind of work*.

Out in the light, the clean air,
crouched against a wall at break
it crept in on me, for most of those
on that lunch truck line

it had to be   enough.

Hard to Believe

Back in that summer of 63',
before the end of Camelot,
when the winds of change
would take over the streets,
I was given a Secret Special Handling
clearance to photograph drawings
of weapons systems on their way to war.
Made the rookie mistake of beating
the lead man's best production
my first day on the job.

And I was the one, young and shapely,
chosen to operate the camera
when an in-house film crew showed up.
All the men trying everything,
but the large flood lights came on
whenever the camera moved up and down,
blowing out their shot.

Ignored, an ornament, a prop, I blurt out,
Why don't you just unscrew the light bulbs,
and they are visibly startled,
shocked a girl dared to speak up,
display lateral thinking.

Wild Woman

after Anne Sexton

I have found the warm cave in the woods.

My shadow, four footed,
has slipped the collar of convention.
I swim in the river beneath the river.
Will not trend with passing fads.

Be, *Her Kind.*
Circle round the fire
chant new Amazon songs
speak up the whispers of your wit.

Do not suffer bad actors
pretentious fools
or look for likenesses.
And never ask permission.

Traveling the Midwest

Across these forever level
playing fields you can see
all the white clapboard places
where the same families
have lived as long as porches.
Where at night you can look up
and clearly see the Milky Way.
And if you move there,
they might let your grandchildren
join in their stories.

Still – putting aside
the petty dramas
that enter all our lives,
here they pitch in,
help a neighbor in need,
and try to keep it simple
like their traffic-free
highways that stretch out
like a ruler to the horizon.
They have always worked hard,
don't complain too much,
and would never ask
for handouts, only jobs.

Exit Interview

Finally, I arrive at the end of work days
Words, so important to be said, get fainter.
The alarm clock plays taps. After fifty years
you enter the Devil's workshop.

When I began on this HR road
employees smoked at their desks,
women could not to take the lead,
harassment was not against the law.

Never Catbert, I celebrated birthdays,
arranged wedding/baby showers, went to wakes.
Ran holiday parties, company picnics,
bus trips to ball games, the theatre.

Now, the Exit Interview classic question,
What did you like most about your job?
And the 98% answer   the people.
Some stay with me!

Like how I could not help but
make it personal, raising the issue
of her smell, and instructing
frequent washings were required
when you work inside an office.

Had to halt the employee,
recently come off the Bible Belt,
from planting religious tracts
for our sorely needed salvation
around a lunchroom full of diversity.

The only met on the phone hearty laugh

of a regional field sales soldier
who dies of a heart attack, alone
in his motel room, at age forty-three.

I saw it all shift in the eighties
when the smart money figured out
they could acquire older companies,
shutter them, and throw whole towns
out of work, to raid the *lazy* assets
in their overfunded pension plans.

Can't forget that haunting walk through ninety years
of oil soaked into a vast wooden floor full of screw holes
where rows and rows of machines had been
to bring *the package* for a redundant executive
who had walked in here at eighteen, now fifty-eight.
I hear his sobbing fill the room.

Once, fired the HR nightmare.
A diesel mechanic loner, over thirty,
who warned a coworker not to come in
to work on this certain date.
I believe what saved us was he came in
a company truck full of his own tools
and it was only right I drive him home,
two hours away, through my most important
listening to his very troubled life,
going seventy mph down the NJ Turnpike.

And then there was old Ben, who
always called me Miss Coleen,
as was the custom from down South.
Who went about his cleaning
with the look of eagles in his eyes
and knew the rivers Langston spoke of.

Had to terminate a veteran branch manager
(worsening alcoholism) with a list of treatment options
that could get him back his job. But just a month later
he took a gun, went into his backyard and ended it all.
We rescued his beloved bulldog with nowhere to go
who wandered through the shop
helping longtime workers grieve.

And of course, there is always an a-hole boss.
He came from a world of sixty thousand employees to our
small town of six thousand. He began by carefully hanging
his twenty-five award plaques from that culture meaningless
to us.

Will never forget meeting Christ Miller,
leading his Mennonites who rode bikes
to our dump-truck plant in Winesburg, Ohio.
My first clue was his statement
this was not a Sherwood Anderson story;
which proceeded to a lunch discussion
of Jefferson and the Constitution
I could have had with my law professor.
Ah yes, my career of trains,
planes and rental cars,
of expensing memorable meals.
Always trying to fit myself
into the square holes of those
quotidian tasks, scrolling through
the ever-changing alphabets
COBRA, EEOC, OSHA.
New forms spitting out of printers,
training bullets peppered on power points.

Now, a file folder I have been here,
the org chart, losing my name.

A Shift

From the solid tasks
of lists   projects   goals
get the ball rolling   deadlines

The total focus
on that   cliff edge
where you're   out of time

Now I have all day
plant flowers   pull weeds
put words   on empty pages.

Have a different
argument with time.

The Lesson

We were on one of many lines
that day of bright colors at Great Adventure.
This one was time for lunch,
when a slightly taller boy on the next line over
began spitting on my grandson.
His mother (rather often I suspect)
obliviously engaged with her friend.

I quickly bent down right into his face
and gave him what my children call
the look of death and in my toughest voice
said, *You better not do that again.*
Then turned, caught up with my line
and left him shaken.

After the balancing of trays we settled
down at our table sorting out the food
when the two storm-filled women approached
and the mother spewed forth a diatribe
about frightening her child. I in my silent Spock
gave her a *what planet are you from* stare.
And she delivered her final coup de mot *bitch*!

I turn to my five-year-old grandson
who has witnessed this entire scene,
and Socratically ask him,
Why didn't Nana say anything?
Then tell him, *Remember, it takes two
people to have an argument.*

Note, to Grandson

You become a teen on this birthday
and we wish for you resilience
as you feel your hormones rising
the ever pressures of making high grades
the awkward truths of superficial friends
and enter the unavoidable darkness
of rebellions ahead.

We unleveled the playing field
as we watched you try on your life,
providing music lessons,
a brown belt in Karate,
summer camp cartooning.
Shared memberships at the Met, MoMA
and the Philadelphia Museum,
trips to seven National Parks,
five historic battlefields, two President's homes,
and all of Washington, DC.
Took you to visit sea life at the Georgia Aquarium,
Sue the dinosaur at the Field Museum,
all those strange animals at so many zoos.
To see Matilda and Hamilton on Broadway.

Yet, more important,
we ask tough questions like,
Is this behavior going to
get you what you want?
Make time to really listen
as we try to keep your baggage light.
Often point to our sign on the wall
that says, *Someone else is happy*
with less than what you have.

Revisiting Frost

Copies of his poems could not
be ready for our next class.
I went and found Frost again
in my bookcase, now full
of alphabetic poets.

It was the book of everything
I had not looked at in many years.
The complete works, and there,
filling the front cover,
he had written eloquently
what I meant to him,
Love Steve, 12-73.

That first marriage
not yet feeling frost.

How Do You Think of It?

It seems that same frozen January 23rd
when the breath of a goodbye is visible.
Yet it's been thirty-nine years since I left
and now   on this January 24th
they tell me you are gone.

How do you think of it,
those years of togetherness?
That last year of High School
when we   two virgins
entered the dating game
which in the early sixties
had to end   and did,
in the white wedding.

I can remember thinking,
literally walking down the aisle
that there was no magic here for me.
But hey, what did I know
that was probably only in books
and I was really fond of this good man,
plus they're not sending
married men to Vietnam.

And now today   how do you think of it?
Those dozen years of marriage
when we had our children,
built a home   grew up.
I became President of the PTA
was elected to the Board of Education.
You went bowling.

And then the one,
the one I thought only in books
showed up!

Crossing Paths 1975

You said it was *bashert*.
That people come our way
for a reason – fate.

Both of us at the southern conference,
not the one I should have been at,
our ages divided by a generation.

You swam into that sea of beige leisure suits
in an open flashy shirt like Fire Island
with long curly hair and a shoulder bag.

I could see the energy, sense those vibes
all the way across the room.
You were on the make.

That night the hotel bar was into swing,
the music I had heard when playing blocks.
You knew all the steps.

And we talked our truths into the night
around the rim of a glass of gin
healing the wound of aloneness.

It cannot be arbitrary, changing
everything just an accident.
Be with me, you said.

At Ninety-One

Reversals may come at any time.

Today, a brief stroke
that sent language
to the land of gibberish,
the body out of balance,
and we are speeding to the ER
where they lay you down,
pull up the rails.

And each new white coat
repeats the same questions
your illness is known for.
Orders tests to peer into
your brain, your heart
pull stories from your blood.

And we all wait – wait
for results, as they search
for the right care,
the right chemistry,
to keep your kisses
with me still.

Frail

You can no longer
attune to gravity's pull.
Now, roll along in a walker
near the edge of life.
Each morning,
muscle memories are
braced at the knees.
Vision, narrowing the field,
blurs available light
while billions of stars
are invisible as always.

Ardor still visits,
and gratitude flows
from your smile,
your kisses.
At this morning's
rousing I say,
*Let's get this show
on the road.*
You tell me,
I want the matinee.

Don't Ask Me to Remember

At this late age some cells
have decided to drop out.
I am your calendar,
fill in the names of things
or repeat myself when
you ask again questions
meant to help you navigate
then moor yourself
in the here, the now.

At times, when I lose patience
say, *But I told you,*
there comes that teasing twinkle
in those soft blue eyes
as you tell me,
But that was an hour ago, or
I've napped since then,
and our laughter comes.

Acknowledgments

A few of my poems have appeared in the following anthologies, some in earlier versions or with different titles: *The Anthologist*, The First of May; *A Hard Turn*, Don Quixote; *A Different Latitude*, Civilities; *US1 Worksheets*, The Bucket and the Dipper.

My forever remembrance of and gratitude to Professor Alicia Suskin Ostriker, who first set me on this path of poetry, and to Mark Doty, whose several workshops and pointed feedback affirmed I was on the right path. I would not have come this far without the US1 Poet's Cooperative critique group, The Delaware Valley Poets, and the Osher Lifelong Learning Institute, Rutgers University.

I am indebted to many kind and thoughtful readers who helped early on and throughout the long development of this manuscript–firstly, Elena Stolzer, Arlyne Desena, June Scharf, Peter Cancro, Gyuri Hollosy, Denise Higgins, and my sister, Lynn Brown. My deepest gratitude to our Four Friends Poetry group, whose insights were invaluable, Enriqueta Carrington, Ilene Millman, and especially Maxine Susman, whose excellent workshops over these past years have inspired many of these poems.

Many thanks to the team at, PrintPOD Publishing, Jacqueline Flamm, Mike Aslett, and Kymberly Rosenthal for skillfully helping a newbie through all this.

Finally, my deepest gratitude to Adolf Konrad, my first mentor, and an amazing artist who created the lovely pastel study of a much younger version of myself now on the cover.

www.ingramcontent.com/pod-product-compliance
Lightning Source LLC
Chambersburg PA
CBHW022000290426
44108CB00012B/1149